Double Challenge

BEING LGBTQ AND A MINORITY

DOUBLE CHALLENGE
BEING LGBTQ AND A MINORITY

By Rebecca Kaplan and Avery Kaplan

Mason Crest
Philadelphia • Miami

Mason Crest
450 Parkway Drive, Suite D
Broomall, PA 19008
(866) MCP-BOOK (toll free)
www.masoncrest.com

Series ISBN: 978-1-4222-4273-5
Hardcover ISBN: 978-1-4222-4276-6
E-book ISBN: 978-1-4222-7523-8

Cataloging-in-Publication Data is available on file at the Library of Congress.

Developed and Produced by Print Matters Productions, Inc. (www.printmattersinc.com)

Cover and Interior Design by Tim Palin Creative

QR CODES AND LINKS TO THIRD-PARTY CONTENT

CONTENTS

KEY ICONS TO LOOK FOR

WORDS TO UNDERSTAND: These words, with their easy-to-understand definitions, will increase readers' understanding of the text while building vocabulary skills.

SIDEBARS: This boxed material within the main text allows readers to build knowledge, gain insights, explore possibilities, and broaden their perspectives by weaving together additional information to provide realistic and holistic perspectives.

EDUCATIONAL VIDEOS: Readers can view videos by scanning our QR codes, providing them with additional educational content to supplement the text.

TEXT-DEPENDENT QUESTIONS: These questions send the reader back to the text for more careful attention to the evidence presented there.

RESEARCH PROJECTS: Readers are pointed toward areas of further inquiry connected to each chapter. Suggestions are provided for projects that encourage deeper research and analysis.

SERIES GLOSSARY OF KEY TERMS: This back-of-the-book glossary contains terminology used throughout this series. Words found here increase the reader's ability to read and comprehend higher-level books and articles in this field.

I'm so excited that you've decided to pick up this book! I can't tell you how much something like this would have meant to me when I was in high school in the early 2000s. Thinking back on that time, I can honestly say I don't recall ever reading anything positive about the LGBTQ community. And while *Will & Grace* was one of the most popular shows on television at the time, it never made me feel as though such stories could be a reality for me. That's in part why it took me nearly a decade more to finally come out in 2012 when I was 25 years old; I guess I knew so little about what it meant to be LGBTQ that I was never really able to come to terms with the fact that I was queer myself.

But times have changed so much since then. In the United States alone, marriage equality is now the law of the land; conversion therapy has been banned in more than 15 states (and counting!); all 50 states have been served by an openly LGBTQ-elected politician in some capacity at some time; and more LGBTQ artists and stories are being celebrated in music, film, and on television than ever before. And that's just the beginning! It's simply undeniable: *it gets better.*

After coming out and becoming the proud queer person I am today, I've made it my life's goal to help share information that lets others know that they're never alone. That's why I now work for the It Gets Better Project (www.itgetsbetter.org), a nonprofit with a mission to uplift, empower, and connect LGBTQ youth around the globe. The organization was founded in September 2010 when the first It Gets Better video was uploaded to YouTube. The viral online storytelling movement that quickly followed has generated over 60,000 video stories to date, one of the largest collections of LGBTQ stories the world has ever seen.

Since then, the It Gets Better Project has expanded into a global organization, working to tell stories and build communities everywhere. It does this through three core programs:

- **Media.** We continue to expand our story collection to reflect the vast diversity of the global LGBTQ community and to make it ever more accessible to LGBTQ youth everywhere. (See, itgetsbetter.org/stories.)
- **Global.** Through a growing network of affiliates, the It Gets Better Project is helping to equip communities with the knowledge, skills, and resources they need to tell their own stories. (See, itgetsbetter.org/global.)
- **Education.** It Gets Better stories have the power to inform our communities and inspire LGBTQ allies, which is why we're working to share them in as many classrooms and community spaces we can. (See, itgetsbetter.org/education.)

You can help the It Gets Better Project make a difference in the lives of LGBTQ young people everywhere. To get started, go to www.itgetsbetter.org and click "Get Involved." You can also help by sharing this book and the other incredible volumes from the LGBTQ Life series with someone you know and care about. You can also share them with a teacher or community leader, who will in turn share them with countless others. That's how movements get started.

In short, I'm so proud to play a role in helping to bring such an important collection like this to someone like you. I hope you enjoy each and every book, and please don't forget: *it gets better.*

Justin Tindall
Director, Education and
Global Programming
It Gets Better Project

**IT GETS
BETTER
PROJECT**

INTRODUCTION

There are members of the lesbian, gay, bisexual, transgender, and questioning (LGBTQ) community living all over the world. LGBTQ people come from every background imaginable, take part in countless careers and callings, and are active and celebrated members of communities. There are many different identities that are covered under the LGBTQ umbrella.

It is possible that this book is your first introduction to the LGBTQ community. Perhaps you have a friend or family member who is part of the LGBTQ community, or you identify as LGBTQ yourself. This book is meant to offer everyone a guide to the double challenge faced by LGBTQ people who embody more than one minority identity that is marginalized.

Many of the ideas that help us understand the multiple challenges that LGBTQ people with intersectional identities must overcome are based on important philosophical and sociological works. One of the influential philosophers who contributed to our understanding of identity politics was a gay man named Michel Foucault. He argued that societal norms perpetuate themselves by forcing people to conform to expected roles to avoid negative social consequences from their peers. People eventually begin to internalize the judgment of others, and they begin to police themselves in a never-ending attempt to match the normative ideal.

Due to these pressures, members of the LGBTQ community sometimes find themselves facing additional challenges. In some instances, these challenges come from discrimination that occurs when a person decides to treat another person in a specific manner because they perceive that person to be a member of the LGBTQ community. In other words, the person becomes the target of discrimination because they were perceived to be LGBTQ. Not only can this treatment be extremely painful in the moment, but it can also cause long-lasting damage to a person's well-being.

However, every person embodies multiple identities. An LGBTQ person's identity comprises more elements than being a member of the LGBTQ community. The nature of each person's identity is a unique combination of variables and singular experiences. This idea was explored by Gloria Evangelina Anazaldúa, who described herself as embodying feminist, mestiza (of spanish and indigenous descent), and lesbian identities in her well-known 1987 book *Borderlands/La Frontera: The New Mestiza*. Anazaldúa writes about her life on the Mexico–Texas border and explores the borderlands formed within herself by the different identities she embodied. In one passage, the various aspects of her identity are compared to distinct people standing on different banks of a river, each one shouting to be heard at the same time.

LGBTQ people may face additional discrimination for other aspects of their identity when they embody more than one marginalized identity. This might mean many different things—LGBTQ women, LGBTQ people of color, and LGBTQ people with a disability. While it is impossible to make a complete list of groups who are marginalized, all of them have LGBTQ members.

When an LGBTQ person is also a member of another marginalized group, they may find themselves facing additional challenges because of their intersecting identities. For example, LGBTQ people who are members of another marginalized group are more likely to experience discrimination. In these cases, the individual may face compounding discrimination, as they are subjected to discriminatory treatment for their LGBTQ identity as well as other identities they may embody. On top of compounded types of discrimination, the interaction of multiple identities can sometimes cause new and unique issues that the individual must face.

A person with identities that embody multiple, distinct marginalized groups must navigate many challenges as they interact with the world. These challenges can be better understood through the framework of intersectionality, which is a concept that is explained by Kimberlé Crenshaw. (See Chapter 1 for more on the conceptual history of intersectionality.) The idea of intersectionality states that the discrimination a person may face can vary, even when compared to other people who have common ground regarding certain aspects of their identity. For example, the way that a white LGBTQ person experiences discrimination may be different from the way an LGBTQ person of color experiences discrimination.

In her original article on intersectionality, Crenshaw illustrates the concept with the idea of a traffic intersection. The cars that are traveling in one direction represent discrimination based on race, while those that travel in a perpendicular direction represent discrimination based on gender. When a black woman is facing discrimination, she is in the middle of intersection, and the injury she receives might come from either direction, or from both at the same time. When an LGBTQ person of color faces discrimination, the injury they receive might originate from their race, their status as an LGBTQ person, or from both directions simultaneously.

In this book, the ways that LGBTQ people with intersectional identities that are different from the norm face a double—or even triple or more—challenge is explored. This work would not have been possible without the ideas and work done by the individuals mentioned by name in this book, as well as those of many countless others.

A note on the language: when it comes to someone's identity, it is important to listen to who they say they are and use the terminology they request. In some cases, a term or label may be widely accepted at one point but considered offensive as time goes by. Throughout this book, we have endeavored to utilize the language we feel best represents the individuals to whom we are referring, but it is not always possible to place historical figures into our current cultural understanding of identity. As two queer women, we hope that any offense will be recognized as unintentional. If you are not certain how a person would like to be identified, it is always best to respectfully ask what language they would like you to use.

LGBTQ people with intersectional identities that are different from the norm face a double—or even triple or more—challenge.

1

UNDERSTANDING INTERSECTIONALITY

WORDS TO UNDERSTAND

DOMINANT VIEW: *The established and controlling cultural perspective.*

NORMATIVITY: *The set of standards to which individuals are expected to conform based on certain characteristics that they may possess, which have been identified as controlling by the dominant view.*

PRIVILEGE: *The benefits that accompany possessing one of the characteristics that characterize the dominant view of normativity.*

TOKENISM: *The process of including members of an underrepresented group to make it appear that the organization includes a full array of perspectives, even though everyone's individual thoughts and values are not fully represented by the organization.*

A lesbian, gay, bisexual, transgender, or questioning person faces a specific set of challenges when interacting with the world due to their sexual orientation and gender. In some cases, this means that people assume that a person will act a certain way or make a certain decision because that person is LGBTQ. In other instances, a person may be treated a certain way because they are perceived to be LGBTQ. However, when an individual's identity includes membership in an additional

A lesbian, gay, bisexual, transgender, or questioning person faces a specific set of challenges.

A black lesbian woman deals with sexism, homophobia, and racism.

minority group as well as LGBTQ group membership, they may face double challenges, or more, due to their intersecting identities. To understand the challenge of belonging to two or more minority groups, it is important to understand the specific challenges these people face day to day. Acknowledging the way that multiple identities can lead to complex and unique issues is an essential component in accomplishing this goal.

THE MANY FACETS OF IDENTITY

Intersectionality can be thought about in a lot of ways. Examples can help to understand the idea.

A woman deals with sexism.
A lesbian woman deals with sexism and homophobia.
A black woman deals with sexism and racism.
A black lesbian woman deals with sexism, homophobia, and racism.

The disadvantages associated with an identity may still affect the individual in the other community in which they might otherwise claim membership. For example, a black lesbian woman will often have to deal with both racism from inside the LGBTQ community and sexism and homophobia in the black community.

In addition, these identities can combine to create trends within certain intersecting groups that may appear "anomalous" when compared to trends common with those who claim membership in any of the individual minority groups to which the LGBTQ person claims membership.

People with an intersectional identity can sometimes feel as though they do not fit in anywhere.

One way that having more than one minority identity that does not match with the expectations set by the **dominant view** is that the individual still experiences the disadvantages of both minority groups. Like the black lesbian woman mentioned above, she deals with the disadvantages caused by sexism, homophobia, and racism. In other words, the disadvantages that affect one aspect of one's identity may still be present within other communities in which they might otherwise be able to claim membership.

People with an intersectional identity can sometimes feel as though they do not fit in anywhere, which can lead to feelings of depression, isolation, and other mental health issues.

By identifying and analyzing the issues that people with intersectional identities face, it is possible to ensure that everyone is included in their communities without having to compromise the unique details that define who they are.

Black women face discrimination on multiple fronts.

The ABCs of intersectionality.

INTERSECTIONALITY: A CONCEPTUAL HISTORY

The term *intersectionality* was coined by Kimberlé Crenshaw in her essential 1989 article "Demarginalizing the Intersection of Race and Sex: A Black Feminist Critique of Antidiscrimination Doctrine, Feminist Theory and Antiracist Policies." By examining several legal decisions, the article demonstrates how black women face discrimination on multiple fronts, as they must cope not only with the sexism that is directed toward all women, but also with the racism that is directed toward all black people. Further, the intersection of multiple identities (in this case, being black and a woman) can create additional and unique issues for a person.

HOW RACISM AFFECTS LGBTQ PEOPLE

The work done by Crenshaw, a professor of law at UCLA and Columbia Law School, on intersectionality has provided the foundation for studying the double challenge faced by LGBTQ people who are also members of other minority groups. Her groundbreaking work articulated how individuals do not fit into neat little boxes but have multiple distinct aspects of their identity that might not fit **normative** expectations. Her work on critical race theory and intersectionality gave the concept its name and provided a framework for the discussion on the unique challenges faced by people with intersecting identities.

LGBTQ people who are also members of other minority groups face multiple challenges.

When a person is a member of a racial minority, they may become the target of discrimination based on their race and appearance. This pressure can seem like a constant presence that affects their navigation through the world daily. However, in some instances, individuals find comfort in other members of the racial minority to which they belong.

A person who is both LGBTQ and a person of color can face additional complications and challenges. When a LGBTQ person faces discrimination within their communities because of their sexual orientation or gender, it can transform a space that might otherwise provide a reprieve from the stress of not aligning with normative expectations into yet another challenge that must be navigated.

Individuals who are members of two or more minority groups may feel pressured to prioritize their different identities.

Individuals who are members of two or more minority groups may feel pressured to prioritize their different identities; for example, they might feel as though they fit in better with peers in their marginalized ethnic group if they conceal the fact that they are LGBTQ. In some instances, those individuals who claim membership in multiple minority communities may find themselves being subjected to the implication that a failure to make a compromise on a specific

Marsha P. Johnson is one of the people credited with instigating the Stonewall Riots.

MARSHA "PAY IT NO MIND" JOHNSON

Marsha P. Johnson was a black trans woman who lived on the streets of New York City until she became a prominent drag queen and LGBTQ rights activist. On June 28, 1969, Marsha was celebrating her birthday at the Stonewall Inn when the police raided the establishment with a warrant for selling liquor without a license. When officers began arresting and harassing LGBTQ patrons, the gay community and its allies began to gather outside the inn as they watched drag queens, lesbians, and other patrons being violently handled by the police before being shoved into police cars. Marsha was one of the first patrons to resist the police that night, so she is credited as being one of the instigators of the Stonewall Riots. She also established the Street Transvestite (now Transgender) Action Revolutionaries with Sylvia Rivera, a trans woman who was among the first in the crowd of onlookers to start rioting at Stonewall. The group helps homeless transgender youth of color in New York City. On July 2, 1992, she was tragically murdered at age 46. Her life and contributions to LGBTQ equality are celebrated in numerous films and books.

point will cost them the progress they have made in being recognized as a valued member of the community.

LGBTQ AND DISABILITY

The LGBTQ community intersects with the disabled community just like it intersects with every other minority group. In the United States, 3 to 5 million people with disabilities identify as LGBTQ. The term *disability* encompasses a wide variety of health conditions that can affect a person's cognitive, emotional, physical, psychological, and sensory abilities. A disability can be either visible or invisible. Unfortunately, sexual orientation is a significant indicator of disability. According to the National Center for Biotechnology Information, lesbian, gay, and bisexual adults have a higher prevalence of disability than their heterosexual peers. Thirty-six percent of lesbian and bisexual women experience some form of disability, compared to 25 percent of heterosexual women. Forty percent of bisexual men and 26 percent of

LGBTQ adults have a higher prevalence of disability than their heterosexual peers.

Discover how the Stonewall Riots began the gay liberation movement in America.

gay men experience a form of disability, compared to 22 percent of heterosexual men. Lesbians and bisexual people were also found to have a higher rate of disability. What's more, LGBTQ individuals are more likely to become disabled at a younger age than their heterosexual peers.

It is important for prevention efforts to understand why LGBTQ people have an increased risk of disability and become disabled at a younger age. According to research, disparities in chronic health conditions, poor physical and mental health, and health risk behaviors among lesbian, gay, and bisexual adults might all be elements that contribute to more LGBTQ people experiencing disability. Health conditions such as arthritis, obesity, and asthma are major contributors. Risky behaviors, such as smoking or a lack of exercise, may also affect the rates of disability among LGBTQ people.

Some famous LGBTQ people with disabilities include CNN anchor Anderson Cooper, who is dyslexic.

In many ways, disability is very much a part of the LGBTQ experience, though it is too often not recognized as such. The LGBTQ community needs to address this subject. Many people with disabilities are active members of the LGBTQ community. Some famous LGBTQ people with disabilities include comedian Stephen Fry (bipolar disorder), CNN anchor Anderson Cooper (dyslexia), political activist Justin Chappell (wheelchair user), artist Frida Kahlo (polio and spinal and pelvis damage), model Aaron Philip (cerebral palsy), and journalist Melissa Yingst (deaf). These celebrities are changing how people think about disability and are great role models for young people with disabilities.

The economy is the strongest when everyone can participate in the workplace. People with both invisible and visible disabilities can be some of the highest achievers on earth. It is important for LGBTQ youth to have positive role models who are members of both these communities. When a group is fighting for its rights, such as the LGBTQ community, it is easy to forget to include people with disabilities in the discussion. By the same token, disability rights organizations often leave the LGBTQ community out of the discussion.

The voices of many with marginalized identities, such as older LGBTQ people, have been poorly represented.

ACKNOWLEDGING PRIVILEGE

When a person possesses an element of their identity that fits into one of the categories widely considered to be normative by the dominant view, that individual possesses privilege. Much of the research conducted by Peter Hegarty has analyzed how norms and **normativity** affect the development of LGBTQ individuals.

The LGBTQ and feminist movements have not always considered intersectional issues and concerns. One frequent criticism of feminist movements, articulated by Audre Lorde in her essay "Age, Race,

Class, and Sex: Women Redefining Difference," is that the principles of feminism only considered the differences in the way that white women are treated when compared to white men, without considering the concerns faced exclusively by women of color. Because this branch of feminist theory is only concerned with issues that originate from gender and not those that might be the result of race, the concerns that women of color need to see addressed go unnoticed, making resolution impossible.

When a person can acknowledge that they possess a certain privilege, they have taken the first step toward recognizing that not everyone enjoys that same privilege. The idea of **privilege** is also discussed by Peggy McIntosh in "White Privilege and Male Privilege: A Personal Account of Coming to See Correspondences Through Work in Women's Studies." In the essay, McIntosh compares the privilege enjoyed by men to an "invisible knapsack" full of useful but unacknowledged tools. McIntosh then discussed the idea that as a white woman, she possesses a similar "invisible knapsack," thanks to her own white privilege.

Recognizing Intersecting Identities

It's important to recognize that there are many different possible aspects of a person's identity, even if some or none of them are immediately apparent to an outside perspective. The voices of many with marginalized identities have been poorly represented, and as such, it is imperative to ensure that their voices are amplified. There are many whose voices need amplification, including but not limited to people with impairments or disabilities, people with non-visible disabilities, overweight people, low-income people, homeless people, people without legal documentation, people from unrepresented or misrepresented religions, and people who are discriminated against because of their age.

Allies may be in the best position to help LGBTQ people who do not enjoy the same privileges.

USING YOUR PRIVILEGE TO HELP

Persons who are members of the LGBTQ community may find themselves facing certain disadvantages because of their identity. But just because a person is disadvantaged in one aspect of their identity does not mean they are universally disadvantaged. By acknowledging privilege, allies will be in the best position to help LGBTQ people—who do not enjoy the same privileges—achieve more equality.

The process of making organizations safe and comfortable for everyone can mean asking difficult questions about fundamental elements, such as how the organization is run and who is fully represented by being invited to make meaningful contributions. If a certain group is not represented within an organization, why is that? In some instances, it may be tempting to write off the lack of inclusion for easy and dismissive reasons. But, while it can be tempting to claim that the reason someone is not included is because they are not present in one's community, it is necessary to take the next step and consider why that group is not represented in the community, and consider what might be done to better ensure that everyone feels welcomed.

Building inclusive organizations is an ongoing process, and it is important to recognize that including everyone is not necessarily a single goal that can be achieved and then filed away as completed. By striving to maintain an inclusive environment through an ongoing and conscious effort to better amplify all voices, one can approach the goal of sustaining a truly welcoming community.

Avoiding **tokenism** is key. When minority voices are included only as nominal or superficial participants, or their opinions are valued only when they align with the views of the majority, the organization has failed to fully include the minority voices. By seriously considering dissenting voices and treating the views of those who speak with respect, the organization can be refined and begin making significant improvements.

One of the practical ways to help ensure that your organization is as inclusive as possible, mentioned by Briannah Hill, a GLAAD Campus Ambassador for the University of Colorado at Boulder, in their article "Three Tips to Make Sure Your Campus Activism Is Intersectional," is to check for possible schedule conflicts with other campus organizations. Hill explains that it is essential that students with intersectional identities not be forced to choose between or among the different identities they embody. Using the example of a pride meeting that occurs at the same time as a Black Student Union to illustrate the potential conflict, they recommend choosing a different night for the meeting or perhaps contacting the organization with the conflicting meeting to see whether a joint coalition of students might be arranged.

When minority voices are included only as superficial participants in an organization, the organization has failed.

TEXT-DEPENDENT QUESTIONS

1. What is one of the important ideas that Kimberlé Crenshaw added to the conversation about intersecting identities?

2. In her essay "White Privilege and Male Privilege," Peggy McIntosh discusses the "invisible knapsack" created by privilege. Do you possess privilege? What is it? What is one thing you can do to help amplify the voices of those who might not possess that privilege?

RESEARCH PROJECTS

1. Marsha P. Johnson played an important role in LGBTQ history. Research some contributions of trans women of color to social justice movements. Did you learn anything surprising? Any responses or reflections?

2. Brianna Hill's article "Three Tips to Make Sure Your Campus Activism Is Intersectional" has some suggestions on ways organizations can ensure they are working to be accessible to everyone. What are some ways that your local organizations can work toward a more welcoming environment for everyone?

2

Race, Ethnicity, and Culture

WORDS TO UNDERSTAND

CISGENDER: *A person whose gender identity and expression matches the gender that they were assigned at birth.*

HOMOPHOBIA: *Discrimination directed toward persons because they are gay or bisexual or otherwise do not conform to normative heterosexual expectation.*

MARGINALIZE: *Regarding the needs or existence of a group of people as irrelevant or secondary to the needs of the majority.*

MENTAL HEALTH: *The condition of the emotional and psychological well-being of a person.*

One of the keys to understanding the double challenge of being both LGBTQ and a member of a **marginalized** group is the complicated interaction between or among intersecting identities. In some

Persons who would otherwise be welcome within a marginalized community can face discrimination because they are LGBTQ.

instances, this can result in a person dealing with the challenges that LGBTQ people face while simultaneously dealing with the challenges faced by individuals in the other marginalized groups to which they claim membership. In other instances, the interaction between the multiple elements that comprise their identity can create unique challenges. Further, in some instances, a person who otherwise would be welcome within a marginalized community faces discrimination because of their status as an LGBTQ individual.

The reasons for this type of reaction are complicated, and may be unique to the specific marginalized group in question. It is essential to recognize that it is impossible to fully understand the identity and challenges that characterize a marginalized group when one cannot claim membership among their number. Therefore, it is important to listen to everyone's voice to ensure that the needs of every individual are met.

LGBTQ people of color may face homophobia from their own ethnic group.

DIFFERENT COMMUNITIES, DIFFERENT REACTIONS

A large body of research shows that people of color face numerous obstacles such as racism and barriers to equal access to educational and employment opportunities. There is also a body of research that shows LGBTQ people must cope with homophobia, bullying and harassment, familial rejection, and homelessness. What happens when someone identifies as an LGBTQ person of color?

LGBTQ people of color face three distinct oppressive experiences:

1. They face homophobia from members of the racial or ethnic group to which they claim membership.
2. They face racism from members of the LGBTQ community, which is predominantly white.
3. They face homophobia and racism from society at large. Unfortunately, transgender people of color may experience further marginalization due to their gender identity or gender expression.

While LGBTQ persons may feel more accepted in certain spaces, they may still spend part of their time in spaces and communities where they do not feel comfortable being themselves. Conversely, some LGBTQ people may come from communities in which they do not feel comfortable being open about the fact that they are LGBTQ, but may feel enabled to express this aspect of their identity fully in mainstream places. This is known as *multiple-minority stress.*

A 2014 study made a conscious attempt to investigate the impact of multiple-minority stress on LGBTQ youth. The study examines the rates of attempted self-harm among LGBTQ youth and found that LGBTQ youth who were also members of another minority group are more likely to attempt suicide. The study ultimately determined that the likelihood that an LGBTQ youth would consider harming themselves is affected by their ethnic and cultural background.

The study's conscious attempt to consider the issue from an intersectional vantage point allows for a deeper understanding of the issue in generally, as well as a more accurate comprehension of the ways that different racial and ethnic identities can inform how LGBTQ people of color experience discrimination.

Adopting a more inclusive approach will be beneficial for everyone—by collecting additional information from research participants, scientific research will become more comprehensive and

The likelihood that an LGBTQ youth will consider harming themselves is affected by their ethnic and cultural background.

offer deeper insight, thanks to diversity of perspectives and experiences. As we better understand the nature of social relationships, we can work toward making society a better place for all members of the community. To achieve these results, however, it is necessary to gather comprehensive data, including diverse perspectives, that make sure every voice is represented.

LGBTQ youth may be rejected by their community for not conforming to ethno-cultural norms.

DEALING WITH HOMOPHOBIA

Many LGBTQ youth of color rely on other members of their racial or ethnic group for support. However, in some cases, they may be the target of **homophobia** in spaces occupied by members of their own racial or ethnic group. In other instances, they may be rejected by their community for not conforming to ethno-cultural norms on sexual orientation and rigid notions of gender. This rejection can be difficult to deal with when it comes from an organization that the individual previously relied on for support. When the support has been taken away because of anti-LGBTQ discrimination, the pain can cut even deeper, leading to physical and mental health problems.

The church plays a significant role in the day-to-day lives of many black Americans, forming a cornerstone of the cultural experience. According to the National Black Justice Coalition Director of Research and Academic Initiative's Dr. Sylvia Rhue, "The black church is not just a place of spirituality and enlightenment, but a place of empowerment

The African Methodist Episcopal (AME) Church officially condemns same-sex relationships.

for African Americans." Yet, there are some members of the clergy and church who are unwelcoming to LGBTQ members. For example, the African Methodist Episcopal (AME) Church officially condemns same-sex relationships. In 2004, the leader of the AME Church issued a rare public condemnation, striking against marriage equality on the stated basis that same-sex relationships constitute a contradiction of their interpretation of Christian scripture.

The teachings coming out of the black church have a significant impact on the lives of LGBTQ people who belong to that community. Twenty-two percent of black LGBTQ people have reported negative experiences with black heterosexual organizations, and importantly, 43 percent of black LGBTQ people have reported negative experiences in community churches and religious institutions.

Coming out and living authentically despite the possible consequences of societal prejudices can seem like a serious challenge.

However, coming out is even more of a challenge for black LGBTQ Americans, who must also face prejudice and fear within the institution that is at the heart of their community, the church. In many instances, those with authority in these institutions are unwilling to reconsider their position to create a community that is more welcoming to LGBTQ people. The consequences that flow from being denied access to one of the basic pillars of support within a minority community can be devastating.

Coming out despite the possible consequences of societal prejudices is a serious challenge.

A person may find it tempting to conceal or deny the fact that they are LGBTQ to continue to enjoy the support of an organization that excludes LGBTQ people. While the notion of passing to continue to draw support may seem to make sense, it probably will not be as easy as it seems. Ultimately, the LGBTQ person may discover that although they pretend to be someone to enjoy the emotional benefit that comes from community support, the emotional benefit rings hollow when it is not supporting the person's authentic self.

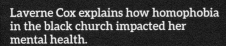

Laverne Cox explains how homophobia in the black church impacted her mental health.

Fundamentalist Christian churches tend to be condemning of LGBTQ people.

RELIGION AND LGBTQ PEOPLE

Some religions do not accept LGBTQ people, and others are only superficially tolerant of LGBTQ members of their congregations. For example, the Church of Latter-day Saints (LDS) does not call for LGBTQ members to be excommunicated as long as they do not act on their attraction. The Roman Catholic Church, the largest Christian denomination in the world, does not officially consider "homosexual orientation" sinful in and of itself, and the Catechism, a text containing the dogmas and teachings of the Church, rejects any form of discrimination against LGBTQ people. However, the Catholic Church has historically had a very negative attitude toward the LGBTQ community and does not allow same-sex marriages or approve of civil unions between same-sex individuals. Fundamentalist Christian churches tend to be even more condemning of LGBTQ people. Some people deal with religious intolerance by creating new churches that maintain the tenants of older institutions, while preaching tolerance of all members, including those who are LGBTQ, while other individuals have created new institutions for worship that are independent and unique from the religious institutions to which they previously belonged.

IMMIGRATION PRESENTS SINGULAR CHALLENGES

LGBTQ people who are also undocumented immigrants face unique challenges. Because LGBTQ undocumented people are at the intersection of two marginalized groups—the LGBTQ community and the undocumented community—they are some of the most vulnerable people.

LGBTQ people who are also undocumented immigrants face unique challenges.

A Williams Institute report estimates there are at least 267,000 LGBTQ adult undocumented immigrants living in the United States. LGBTQ undocumented immigrants are more likely to be male, younger, and Asian than the overall undocumented immigrant population; however, they are less likely to be Hispanic.

The legal challenges faced by LGBTQ people who are also undocumented can come with severe consequences. Even a minor traffic violation or a misdemeanor might mean being transferred to a detention center for surveillance, a prospect that may include solitary confinement for transgender individuals. The disproportionate stakes that accompany such minor infractions contribute to an ever-increasing level of stress. A clear path to citizenship would reduce some of the challenges faced by this community by reducing the risk of deportation.

However, citizenship will not solve all the problems facing the LGBTQ undocumented community. Countless binational families are unable to sponsor same-sex partners through family-based immigration preferences. It is unfair and cruel to force these families to live apart.

LGBTQ immigrants face unique challenges when they go through the immigration enforcement system. To illustrate the difficulties of

Citizenship will not solve all the problems facing the LGBTQ undocumented community.

those who face the double challenge of being an LGBTQ immigrant is the story of a transgender woman detained by the United States Immigration and Customs Enforcement (ICE). Transgender women are often detained in facilities that otherwise exclusively hold men. This was the case for Kripcia, a transgender woman who contacted activist Ruby Corado in 2012. She was sentenced to solitary confinement, the area of the jail where they also confine

Undocumented transgender people face extreme and inhuman punishment.

sex offenders, in a men's facility. ICE justified the confinement based on the claim that it was the only safe way for the guards to provide surveillance for the detained woman.

Corado was skeptical that surveillance concerns made it necessary to keep Kripcia in solitary confinement for 22 hours a day. By the time Kripcia was able to contact Corado, she had spent eight months in an ICE detention center. Kripcia was arrested for failing to pay a cab fare, but due to the double challenge that comes with being a transgender woman and being undocumented, she faced extreme and inhuman punishment as a result.

The official response to these situations is that it is impossible to maintain enough facilities. However, Corado says she has never heard of a transgender detainee who had been treated like a human being while being subjected to immigration detention, which is not intended to be a punishment. Nevertheless, during her time being kept in solitary confinement, Kripcia repeatedly expressed how difficult it was for her to survive the inhuman conditions she faced while incarcerated in Rappahannock Regional Jail.

"Two-spirit" is a unique gender role that exists in some indigenous North American cultures.

Discover the four genders in traditional Navajo culture.

Culturally Unique Gender Roles and Expressions

Gender roles can be culturally unique, like "two-spirit," a role that exists in some indigenous North American cultures. Two-spirit is impossible to understand outside of a framework established many generations in the past, and it cannot be self-applied: the conferral of this ancient and sacred role is the providence of the ceremonial community of the Elder of the Two Spirit. Analogous roles do not appear in all indigenous North American cultures, nor is "two-spirit" necessarily an accurate descriptor. Different manifestations of two-spirit occurring across indigenous North American traditions demonstrate the complex interaction of gender identity and culturally unique roles.

TEXT-DEPENDENT QUESTIONS

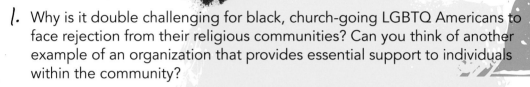

1. Why is it double challenging for black, church-going LGBTQ Americans to face rejection from their religious communities? Can you think of another example of an organization that provides essential support to individuals within the community?

2. Who can adopt the identity of "two-spirit"? Why is the number of people who can claim this identity limited?

RESEARCH PROJECTS

1. Research an LGBTQ-friendly religious organization in your area. Does the organization exclusively cater to LGBTQ people, or is it a universally inclusive group?

2. Depending on where you live, there may be local festivals honoring ethnic and cultural heritage. See whether LGBTQ pride is one of the components included in the festival.

3

Building Community

Double Challenge: Being LGBTQ and a Minority

WORDS TO UNDERSTAND

DISCRIMINATION: *Treating a person differently or unjustly because they are a member of a marginalized community.*

HETERONORMATIVE: *The attitude or assumption that heterosexuality is the normal and natural expression of sexuality and gender, instead of one of many possibilities.*

IDENTITY AFFIRMATION: *The process that helps LGBTQ people develop positive feelings and a sense of belonging in their social group.*

MARGINALIZED COMMUNITIES: *Groups of people who are separated from the majority because they are considered to be different due to their race, culture, gender expression, sexual orientation, or religion.*

LGBTQ people who are also members of other **marginalized communities** face a unique challenge in finding a group that embraces them for who they are. LGBTQ people, like anyone, should be

LGBTQ people should be free to be themselves without facing discrimination.

free to be themselves without facing discrimination. Unfortunately, many members of the LGBTQ community are not accepted by their minority groups. According to statistics gathered by the Human Rights Campaign Foundation, 50 percent of LGBT people of color have experienced discrimination from their ethnic and racial communities, while 45 percent say they have been subjected to harassment within their communities, and 45 percent have been rejected after coming out. For these doubly marginalized people, the personal communities they build can be an invaluable source of support and strength.

SHAME AND SILENCE

LGBTQ people often face **discrimination** in their day-to-day lives, and for those who are also members of other marginalized communities, the challenges they face are that much more difficult. There is a lot of research about individuals who are members of marginalized communities and research about people who identify as LGBTQ; however, there is little research on LGBTQ people who are also members of marginalized communities.

Until there was little research on the experiences of LGBTQ women and people of color.

Until recently, most LGBTQ research focused on white males, and there was little research on the experiences of LGBTQ women and people of color. However, social scientists are beginning to fill in the gaps in the existing literature, thanks to the support of organizations such as the Human Rights Campaign and The Williams Institute.

It is becoming increasingly clear that that those who fall into this double-minority category face a unique set of problems. What's more, each ethnic and racial community has different expected roles and behaviors for their members, and many of these revolve around gender roles. For example, LGBTQ Asian Americans may experience additional stressors because of heterosexism in the Asian American community. Social scientists have suggested that heterosexism is much stronger in Asian and Asian American cultures than it is in the dominant U.S. culture because homosexuality runs counter to traditional Asian values, which tend to dictate that men and women adhere to traditional and stereotypical gender roles.

The situation for Asian American LGBTQ people is illustrated by "Randy," who was interviewed for a study of gay Asian Americans. Today, Randy is a successful nurse, but in high school he faced social isolation. Randy said that he felt he was not accepted by the Asian American community because he was gay, but he also did not feel that there was a place for him in the LGBTQ community because he "did not fit the stereotypical white images of gay culture depicted in the mass media."

When an LGBTQ person is perceived to be violating their community's expectations—because of how they express themselves, the clothes they wear, whom they choose as partners, and what gender roles they play within their families—they may be made to feel like they are wrong for being who they are. This pressure to conform to **heteronormative** roles can lead to LGBTQ persons no longer feeling welcome in the community they were born into.

There is more pressure for LGBTQ people to fulfill heteronormative roles in some communities than in others. In the United States, researchers have demonstrated that black LGBTQ youth experience more pressure to fit into heteronormative roles than their white counterparts. As one gay black man told the Human Rights Campaign, "I think that there was finally a decision somewhere that I made that if I was really going to be gay, if I was going to come out, that was sort of like my exit papers from the black community." Gay, bisexual, or transgender black youth often find themselves needing

It is important to remember that in every community, there will be some members who are accepting.

to navigate communities that simultaneously value one aspect of their emerging identities, while disapproving of another.

It is important to remember, however, that there is diversity in every community. This means that in every community, there will be at least some members who are accepting. It is worth trying to find those supportive members in your community of birth.

LGBTQ people may attempt to adopt a normative identity within their community.

BE TRUE TO YOURSELF

Conforming to the traditional gender and societal roles imposed by their community may seem like an easier option for some LGBTQ people. They may attempt to adopt a normative identity within their community, never sharing their true selves with almost anyone, including their loved ones. They may lead a double life, presenting a normative façade to other members of the community while expressing their true selves in secret, like Josh Weed, a married Mormon man whose wife is aware that he identifies as gay. Still others may conceal who they truly are, even from themselves, refusing to acknowledge their true nature, while never feeling fulfilled with the role they are attempting to perform.

The truth is, a person will never feel truly fulfilled unless they are honest with themselves about who they are and what will make them happy.

Watch the music video "Q.U.E.E.N." by Janelle Monáe.

DON'T JUDGE ME

Janelle Monáe came out as pansexual to help her fans gain the courage to accept themselves for who they are.

Janelle Monáe, an American actress and musician, came out as pansexual to help her fans and listeners gain the courage to accept themselves. In an interview with *People*, Monáe spoke directly to her young fans: "I've always hoped, by sharing my stories that people will feel more comfortable walking in their truths. And feel like it's not a heavy burden, you know, that you do have support." LGBTQ celebrities, like Monáe, have helped to gain acceptance for fluid sexuality. Seeing LGBTQ celebrities living openly as their true selves can give others the confidence to accept their own nature.

DEALING WITH REJECTION

For an LGBTQ person, being rejected by their community is painful and can be devastating. If your parents or guardian kick you out of the house, suddenly, coming out means facing the reality of becoming homeless and the uncertainty of where you will find your next meal. This fear keeps many minority LGBTQ young people from telling their parents until they have moved out of the house. If you think being kicked out of the house is a real possibility, and you still want to come out to your parents, have a safety plan in place. Initial reactions may be strong, and you and your parents may both need time to adjust. Have somewhere lined up where you can be safe during that time. If things do not go well, do not stay where there is a risk of violence. Violence is never an acceptable reaction.

For an LGBTQ person, being rejected by their community can be devastating.

If you find yourself rejected by the community you were born into, professional therapy can help. A therapist or counsellor can help sort through many of the complicated and difficult feelings a person rejected by their community experiences. No matter how hard things get for an LGBTQ person who is facing rejection because of who they are, it is important to remember that there are healthy ways of dealing with every problem, and a mental health professional can help you discover solutions to what may seem like impossible situations.

For many minority groups, the strength of the family is especially important. This can make it that much harder for minority LGBTQ

For many minority groups, the strength of the family is especially important.

people to come out to their loved ones and community. Sometimes, a family may choose to tolerate the LGBTQ person but never allow their identity to be discussed. In these cases, "tolerance is often gained at the price of silence," as Cheryl A. Parks writes in her article "Race/Ethnicity and Sexual Orientation: Intersecting Identities."

When a person is rejected from a marginalized community, they may be more vulnerable to bullying or physical violence. Being an accepted member of a marginalized group can provide protection against attacks or intimidation from people outside the group. When an LGTBQ person is rejected from the group, they also lose those protections. In addition to finding themselves exposed to racism, the person will face discrimination as an LGTBQ person. Being ostracized from their community leaves them particularly susceptible to discrimination and/or abuse.

REDEFINING COMMUNITY

For members of marginalized communities, the kinship they lose when their community rejects them can be devastating. They may not be able to change the community, but they can form new bonds in a new one to help them overcome the challenges of marginalization.

For some people, LGBTQ communities provide much-needed support.

Community is an important part of life. While rejection from a marginalized community can be extremely difficult, it is important for ostracized LGBTQ people to find new communities that accept and embrace them for who they are.

For some people, LGBTQ communities provide much-needed support. There are many welcoming organizations out there. These groups may include all members of the LGBTQ community or cater specifically to lesbians, gay men, transgender women, or other groups.

LGBTQ people may also build informal communities around shared interests and activities. One example is Lavender Light Gospel Choir, the first people-of-all-colors lesbian and gay gospel choir in the United States. Since 1985, Lavender Light has provided LGBTQ people in New York City with a community that revolves around coming together to share a passion and interest in singing gospel music. Choir members do not have to choose between participating in a gay community or a black community. The best way to find community organizations like these is to search online.

If you have a hobby or passion, you may be able to find other LGBTQ people who share your interest, and form your own community. Gay for Good, a nonprofit organization, brings together LGBTQ people to volunteer on projects that benefit the larger community. Gay for Good has opened chapters in cities across the United States and organizes projects that include volunteering at zoos and cleaning up local rivers. Those who enjoy spending time in the great outdoors might consider participating in a group like Unlikely Hikers, an organization started by Jenny Bruso that seeks to unite LGBTQ people with others who enjoy the great outdoors. For some individuals, an LGBTQ-friendly church, synagogue, temple, or mosque group or organization may provide the acceptance and community they seek.

While the organization doesn't have to be exclusively for LGBTQ people, it is essential for LGBTQ people who have faced rejection to find a community that wholly accepts them for who they are. One study found that by exploring their identity with others who shared that identity, people's mental well-being was improved, thanks to **identity affirmation**. Identity affirmation can strengthen the bonds a person feels with other group members and improve their lives in countless ways.

If you have a hobby or passion, you may be able to find other LGBTQ people who share your interest.

Discover the history of ball culture.

Having a Ball

Prominent within ball culture are events at which the houses come together to compete for cash prizes.

The ball culture that emerged during the Harlem Renaissance of the 1920s and 1930s featured black transgender women and gay men performing in drag at large multiracial events. In the 1960s and 1970s, members of the ball community began to form "houses" in large cities across the United States. The community has continued to grow and evolve, becoming an established social structure led by gender-nonspecific house "fathers" or "mothers" who manage the house and provide support to the house "children," or members. Prominent within ball culture are events at which the houses come together to compete for cash prizes and "ball status." In addition to formal houses, there is a "kiki," or family scene, that provides a safe place for LGBTQ youth to practice "vogueing" and other ball-competition skills.

The ball scene thrives, in part, because it serves as an in-group for black and Latino LGBTQ youth who frequently are not accepted in other contexts. As shown by the documentary *Paris is Burning* (about ball culture in New York City) and the FX Network's groundbreaking series *Pose*, these "houses" can offer vital support and a literal roof over the heads of LGBTQ youth of color who otherwise might have become homeless after coming out to their families.

FINDING YOUR TRIBE

When an LGBTQ person has been rejected from the community they were born into, it can be hard for them to imagine they will ever again feel a sense of belonging. The trials faced by those who are ostracized from a marginalized community can seem unbearable, as rejected individuals may lose relationships with family and friends, or find themselves losing membership in religious communities and being subjected to social stigma by their neighbors. While these challenges can seem unbearable, it is important to remember that it is possible to find a new community that will allow you to express yourself fully.

"Discovering your tribe" is a phrase that describes finding others who share a similar worldview and value system. It is important to note, however, that discovering your tribe does not mean losing what makes you unique! One of the best things about building your own community is the opportunity to recognize that shared qualities, such as a commitment to change the world or the desire to form close bonds with one another, can bring people together despite differences in upbringing, heritage, and culture.

It may be tempting to pretend to be something you are not, to feel more accepted within a particular community. But in the long run, happiness will come from being yourself, liking yourself, and feeling accepted just as you are.

"Discovering your tribe" is finding others who share a similar worldview and value system.

TEXT-DEPENDENT QUESTIONS

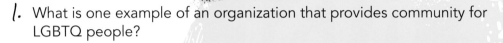

1. What is one example of an organization that provides community for LGBTQ people?

2. What are three possible consequences an LGBTQ person might face if they are rejected from their minority community?

3. What is one way that a LGBTQ person who has been rejected from their minority community can overcome the rejection they face?

RESEARCH PROJECTS

1. What are some of your favorite hobbies and passions? Find a community organization near you for others who share your interests.

2. If you are an ally or a member of the LGBTQ community who is not a member of a marginalized group, think of three ways that you can help LGBTQ people who might not have the same privileges as you. If you are part of a marginalized community, think of three ways that you can help other LGBTQ members of your community.

4

LEGAL ISSUES

ASYLUM: *The protection granted to a person who has left their native country as a refugee.*

DISCRIMINATION: *Discrimination occurs when someone is unjustly deprived of their rights and life opportunities due to negative attitudes or beliefs about a minority group.*

HARASSMENT: *A type of discrimination that includes unwanted physical or verbal behavior that offends or hurts another person.*

Many lesbian, gay, bisexual, transgender, and questioning people across the world have been denied basic rights in their lifetime. Two major factors behind this unfortunate fact are the laws and conventions of society. To this day, there are many nations and states that maintain laws allowing discrimination based on sexual orientation or gender identity. **Discrimination** can result in groups of people being excluded from receiving certain societal benefits—it deprives them of their civil rights, such as access to fair housing opportunities; it creates barriers to pursuing academic goals and securing

Many LGBTQ people around the world have been denied basic rights.

Anti-discrimination laws and policies are intended to improve the situation of marginalized groups.

employment; and it prevents them from spending their lives beside the person of their choosing.

People can experience discrimination due to different aspects of their identity, including but not limited to race, ethnicity, age, gender, or sexual orientation. When people experience discrimination based on more than one aspect of their identity, it can be difficult to predict the impact on the individual. LGBTQ people who are also members of another minority group are more likely to experience discrimination, and thus, it is more likely they will be denied equal access to education, employment, and employment. This is due to inseparable categories of inequality, the effects of which can compound and overlap.

To improve the situation of marginalized groups, anti-discrimination laws and policies strive to address the differences between and within marginalized communities. However, it is difficult to address these differences effectively without invaluable insight and perspective provided by the voices of those who are included within the marginalized groups. Their voices must be heard so that their individual and unique needs may be illuminated and addressed.

HOUSING AND EMPLOYMENT ISSUES

Members of the LGBTQ community experience higher rates of discrimination than their heterosexual and cisgender peers. For example, LGBTQ singles and couples may face discrimination when they buy or rent a home. There is no federal law to prohibit someone refusing to rent or sell to an LGBTQ person solely on the basis of sexual orientation or gender identity.

The establishment of marriage equality as U.S. law in 2015 certainly helped to right some of the abuses, but it only helps LGBTQ couples who choose to marry. In some instances, same-sex couples may undertake additional legal precautions or exploit legal loopholes to safeguard against this eventuality. One benefit provided by marriage is the assurance that, in the unfortunate event that one partner dies, the other will enjoy certain legal protections. During the 20th century in the United States, gay couples faced discrimination in the form of laws that would not allow them to marry their partners. As a result, in the

LGBTQ singles and couples may face discrimination when they buy or rent a home.

event that one partner died, the other partner might find themselves without financial support. Some couples avoided this by having one adult partner legally adopt the other adult partner. This ensured that if one partner died, the other would be provided with legal protection.

LGBTQ people are also subjected to employment discrimination. For example, one in five LGBTQ people reports that they have experienced discrimination because of their sexuality or gender identity when applying for jobs.

The likelihood that an LGBTQ person will face discrimination increases when the person is not white. LGBTQ people of color are twice as likely as white LGBTQ people to say they have been personally discriminated against when applying for jobs because they are LGBTQ.

Almost two-thirds of LGBTQ people of color have experienced discrimination due to their race or ethnicity, and half have experienced discrimination for their sexual orientation or gender expression. Racial discrimination is more commonly experienced by African American LGBTQ people (74 percent) than by either Latinos (54 percent) or Asian Pacific Islanders (60 percent), even though all groups felt equally discriminated against for being LGBTQ.

Almost two-thirds of LGBTQ people of color report having experienced discrimination due to their race or ethnicity.

This demonstrates how the double challenge can affect LGBTQ people of color, that is, increasing the chances that they will face discrimination because of their sexual orientation or gender identity.

LGBTQ people of color are more likely than their white peers to experience discrimination during interactions with the police. Thus, LGBTQ people of color are six times more likely than white LGBTQ people to say they have avoided calling the police due to concern for anti-LGBTQ discrimination.

There are numerous laws to protect LGBTQ people from discrimination, but they vary based on country and jurisdiction. In the United States, some states provide more protections for LGBTQ people than those mandated by the federal government.

For example, under Title VII of the Civil Rights Act of 1964, American employers are prohibited from discriminating against employees based on sex. Several state and federal courts have extended Title VII and other federal sex discrimination laws to transgender people. Federal sex discrimination laws prohibit employers from discriminating based on gender stereotypes.

LGBTQ youth are more likely to be bullied in school.

BULLYING

LGBTQ youth are more likely to be bullied in school. According to the 2017 Youth Risk Behavior Survey, more American high school students who self-identify as lesbian, gay, or bisexual report having been bullied on school property or cyberbullied in the past year than their heterosexual peers. The study also shows that more lesbian, gay, and bisexual students than heterosexual students reported missing school because of safety concerns.

The United States Constitution guarantees equal protection for all, including LGBTQ people.

Youth who are bullied are at increased risk for depression, suicidal ideation, abuse of drugs and alcohol, and risky sexual behavior. Studies show that bullying affects academic performance, and for LGBTQ youth, the risk is even higher. Research has shown that being out as LGBTQ has both beneficial psychosocial and developmental effects for youth. However, being out or just being perceived as being LGBTQ increases the risk of bullying for some youth.

To prevent and address bullying of LGBTQ students in schools it is important to consider their unique situations. Making schools safer benefits every single student. Although some strategies are specifically designed for issues faced by LGBTQ youth, most will benefit the entire student body.

HOW THE LAW PROTECTS LGBTQ YOUTH

While acceptance of LGBTQ people has increased in many places, there is still a great deal of progress to be made, and instances of **harassment** still occur. These incidents can take many forms, from one student bullying another between classes to adults making rude and unsolicited remarks to people in public.

There are laws and policies that prohibit discrimination based on sexual orientation and gender identity. Someone does not have to be out to be protected from anti-LGBTQ discrimination. It is not even necessary to be gay, lesbian, bisexual, transgender, or questioning—discrimination based on perceived sexual orientation or gender identity is unlawful, as is discrimination based on a friendship, family relationship, or association with LGBTQ people.

In the U.S., LGBTQ people are guaranteed equal protection by the laws under the U.S. Constitution as well as many state constitutions. This has several implications for LGBTQ students. It means they cannot

It is essential for LGBTQ students who feel bullied to feel comfortable approaching a teacher.

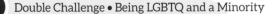

be treated differently because school officials disapprove of being gay or feel uncomfortable around gender non-conforming students. It also means that school officials must take bullying and harassment of LGBTQ students as seriously as they would for any other student.

It is essential for LGBTQ students who feel bullied to feel comfortable approaching a teacher or other member of the school administration so that they no longer are bullied in their school.

One legal protection at the national level in the United States is Title IX, a federal law that protects students against discrimination based on sex at schools receiving federal funding. According to the courts, Title IX prohibits discrimination and sexual harassment for failing to conform to gender stereotypes.

Some states are passing laws that specifically protect LGBTQ youth against discrimination and harassment in schools; however, states vary widely in how they structure, apply, and enforce these laws. There are detailed safeguards in a growing number of states, such as California, Iowa, Maryland, New Jersey, New York, and Vermont. In these states, the law requires local school boards to pass anti-harassment policies that include protections against bullying based on sexual orientation and gender identity. The policies must also set up a system for students to file complaints regarding bullying, and a system that allows those complaints to be investigated.

WHAT LEGAL PROTECTIONS DON'T COVER

One of the major elements of Kimberlé Crenshaw's article "Demarginalizing the Intersection of Race and Sex" is the analysis of three legal decisions involving black women, and how each decision fails to provide the protection needed by black women in each instance. In one decision, the court found that offering a solution that matched the interests of black women would not provide ample protection for the interests of black men in a comparable situation.

Favorable legal decisions don't always provide all the necessary legal protection.

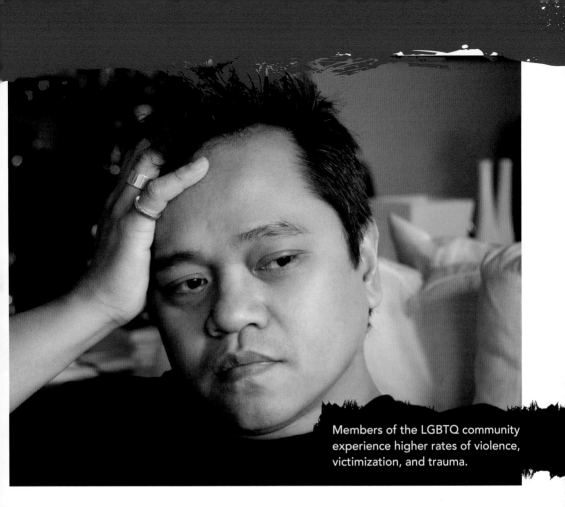

Members of the LGBTQ community experience higher rates of violence, victimization, and trauma.

VIOLENCE, VICTIMIZATION, AND TRAUMA

Members of the LGBTQ community experience higher rates of violence, victimization, and trauma. The violence and trauma can be physical, emotional, verbal, psychological, and sexual. It can happen at home, at school, or in the community. It can come at the hands of a family member, friend, peer, or stranger.

Violence, victimization, and trauma are realities for too many LGBTQ people. Several studies have shown high rates of anti-gay victimization, with one estimating that 80 percent of LGBTQ people experience some form of harassment during their lifetime. Supporting the conclusions of the scientific research, Internet users have posted over 60,000 *It Gets Better* videos detailing their personal experiences with violence against LGBTQ people.

Protection from violence and discrimination are important issues facing LGBTQ people of color. According to the Human Rights Campaign, women are most concerned with safety in their community and for children. Men, on the other hand, share stories of facing violence, sometimes from family members. In Los Angeles, one gay man could not return to Mexico because he feared his father would kill him because of his sexual orientation.

For these doubly marginalized groups, however, discrimination and violence stem more often from race than from being an LGBTQ person. Almost one-third of LGBTQ people of color have experienced race-based violence, and nearly a quarter have suffered violence because of their sexual orientation or gender identity. Among doubly marginalized groups, black LGBTQ people are most likely to have experienced racially motivated violence. Similarly, almost one-third of LGBTQ Asian Pacific Islanders have experienced race-based violence.

Fortunately, in the past several years, more attention has been paid to this epidemic as cultural stances and legal policies continue to change.

Facing Changing Legal Protections

As anti-LGBTQ sentiment is rising across the globe for the first time in several decades, the federal and state legal protections for LGBTQ people are rapidly changing across the United States. It is a tumultuous time for federal legal protections for LGBTQ people living in the United States. The LGBTQ community is starting to lose legal protections that they had won. It is a period of instability for many LGBTQ Americans, and the ultimate outcome is uncertain. Because of this, it is important to stay informed about the status of federal and state legal protections regarding the rights of LGBTQ people. This is not always easy, as one key strategy used by anti-LGBTQ movements involves the suppression of public information regarding the LGBTQ community. Even if you are not old enough to vote, there are ways to make your voice heard and to help ensure that everyone has legal protections and that their rights are preserved.

Anti-LGBTQ sentiment is rising across the globe for the first time in several decades.

Many transgender people flee persecution in their home countries.

IMMIGRATION CHALLENGES

In the United States, immigration law is always changing and always complicated. It can be particularly challenging for lesbian, gay, bisexual, transgender, questioning, and HIV-positive immigrants to navigate because they face unique challenges due to their sexual orientation or gender identity. Some LGBTQ immigrants flee persecution in their home countries or face discrimination in the United States. Other immigrants need help navigating a family-based immigration application or changing their gender marker on official documents.

According to a Williams Institute study, there are an estimated 267,000 undocumented people in the United States who identify as LGBTQ. In addition, many U.S.-born LGBTQ people have documented and undocumented family members, partners, and friends who are impacted by decisions on immigration policy.

Transgender immigrants and **asylum** seekers often find themselves being mistreated when they enter the immigration-detention system. Many transgender people flee persecution in their home countries, and as a result, there are a higher percentage of trans asylum seekers and undocumented transgender immigrants living outside their home countries than many people realize. The National Center for Transgender Equality estimates that between 15,000 and 50,000 undocumented transgender immigrants live in America; however, the number of undocumented transgender immigrants may be higher, as many people are reluctant to self-report as transgender. People often do not self-report as transgender, because they fear being mistreated by U.S. Immigration and Customs Enforcement officials. As a result, they remain in the closet, afraid to live authentically due to the potential repercussions.

There are over 70 countries that have criminalized LGBTQ people, and many more that are extremely difficult places for transgender people to live. One example is the Chechen Republic, a state near Russia that officially denies the existence of LGBTQ people, while imprisoning in concentration camps anyone suspected of being LGBTQ. Concrete statistics on these types of situations abroad can be difficult to obtain, since officials in these countries are unlikely to release accurate details concerning the situation.

When these refugees arrive in the U.S. seeking asylum and safety, they face abuse, discrimination, and mistreatment due to their transgender status. Transgender women are detained in 17 facilities run by U.S. Immigration and Customs Enforcement, but four are otherwise all-male facilities. In addition, there is one transgender "pod" of detainment in Cibola County, New Mexico. Trans women are held in ICE custody for twice as long as other immigrants. According to a 2018 letter from the office of New York's Democratic Representative Kathleen Rice to the Department of Homeland Security (DHS), "of the 298 transgender people ICE detained in fiscal year 2017, 13 percent were placed in solitary confinement."

A transgender person fleeing persecution or maltreatment due to their transgender status can qualify for asylum. However, it can take years to be granted asylum, and many people may ultimately find themselves working hard to navigate a confusing and unfriendly system.

TEXT-DEPENDENT QUESTIONS

1. What is one area where LGBTQ people face discrimination? What happens when the LGBTQ person is also a member of another group that faces discrimination?

2. Why is there a higher-than-average percentage of transgender people who are undocumented immigrants? What complications does this create in the immigration process?

RESEARCH PROJECTS

1. What legal protections are available for LGBTQ people in your area? Are these different from the legal protections available to all LGBTQ people in your country?

2. Research an organization in your area that is working to increase the legal protections available to LGBTQ people or any other marginalized group.

5
WEATHERING THE STORM

a Minority

WORDS TO UNDERSTAND

MINORITY STRESS: *A concept developed by psychologists to describe the unique pressures faced by minority groups.*

STIGMA: *Refers to the attitudes and beliefs that lead people to avoid, fear, or reject others they think are different.*

Lesbian, gay, bisexual, transgender, and questioning people are becoming more accepted by society, and thus they are more able to live as their authentic selves. Despite greater acceptance in many instances, LGBTQ people continue to face **stigma** and discrimination in other situations. LGBTQ individuals may delay or avoid health care and health maintenance screenings they need because of negative

LGBTQ individuals may delay or avoid health care they need because of negative experiences.

Health care providers who are insensitive to LGBTQ issues can make their patients feel invisible.

experiences, such as stigma and discrimination, in a health care setting. As discussed in previous chapters, LGBTQ people of color are more likely to experience discrimination in the health system than their white counterparts, making it more likely that this will constitute a barrier in treatment for those facing this double challenge.

LGBTQ HEALTH CARE DISCRIMINATION

All people who need medical treatment should be able to see a doctor without experiencing stigma or discrimination. However, many communities have limited access to health care that they need. Although there are many different barriers limiting access to health care for members of the LGBTQ community, bias and discrimination of health care providers is one of the most significant barriers.

LGBTQ health care discrimination has become an important topic of debate, in part because it is related to significant functional impairment. Indeed, LGBTQ people are more likely to experience physical and mental health problems due to their frequent experiences with anti-gay stigma and discrimination. For example, a national survey found that lesbian, gay, and bisexual people are at heightened risk of psychological distress, drinking, and smoking, and that lesbian and bisexual women are at heightened risk of having multiple chronic conditions. The little research on transgender individuals in the United States shows they are more likely to be overweight, be depressed, report cognitive difficulties, and forgo treatment for health problems than cisgender people. These health disparities are more common than suicide or homicide and incur significant personal and social costs. It isn't being LGBTQ that causes the increase in these issues— they arise from the social intolerance these individuals have faced.

The potential for discrimination can deter LGBTQ people from seeking necessary medical care. Approximately 6 percent of LGBTQ people said they avoided the doctor in the past year out of fear of discrimination, according to the Center for American Progress. This avoidance behavior was even more common among LGBTQ people who reported having experienced discrimination in the past year, with 18.4 percent of them reporting not going to the doctor, to avoid discrimination. The 2015 U.S. Transgender Survey found that 23 percent of respondents had avoided seeking health care in the past year due to fear of discrimination because of their gender identity.

Unfortunately, instances of individual mistreatment are only part of the problem. When LGBTQ individuals need to access health care, they face many other barriers to accessing it, in addition to discrimination. For example, LGBTQ individuals are twice as likely to be uninsured as the general population, and when they are insured, their policies may exclude necessary medical care. Most health insurance policies still exclude transgender care despite the overwhelming medical consensus on the necessity and benefit of transition-related surgeries for transgender individuals.

LGBTQ individuals often have trouble finding health care providers who will treat their unique needs related to their sexual orientation and gender identity.

The delay or denial or medical care may have serious health consequences for the patient.

Health care providers who are insensitive to LGBTQ issues can make their patients feel invisible. Dismissing same-sex partners as "friends" rather than life-partners or interacting with patients from personal bias and stereotypes can keep LGTBQ people from receiving appropriate medical care.

LGBTQ people of color, specifically, tend to lack access to culturally affirming and informed health care. They are more likely than their white counterparts to experience significant health care discrimination and substandard medical care.

Discrimination in health care settings puts the lives of LGBTQ individuals at risk. When a health care provider refuses to treat a patient because of their sexual orientation or gender identity, the delay or denial or medical care may have serious health consequences for the patient. For example, a patient with HIV reported that after he disclosed to hospital staff that he was gay, they ignored him, refused to allow his family to visit, and did not provide his HIV medication. The doctor at the hospital told the patient's personal doctor, "This is what he gets for going against God's will" and "You must be gay, too, if you're his doctor." The patient missed five doses of his HIV medication because of the treating doctor's biases. A missed or delayed dose can make HIV medicine less effective or even completely ineffective, so it is extremely important that a patient never misses a dose.

Some places have enacted laws to protect transgender people from health-related discrimination.

In many instances, health care concerns must be addressed swiftly, or the potential for irreversible fallout becomes more likely.

GETTING THE CARE YOU NEED

Lesbian, gay, bisexual, transgender, and questioning people are more likely than cisgender heterosexual people to experience problems accessing the health care they need. LGBTQ individuals are less likely than other people to have health insurance, they are more likely to have untreated health needs, and, for woman, they are less likely to undergo important preventive testing for diseases such as breast cancer.

There are resources available to LGBTQ individuals who want to find a health care provider. University-based clinics with training programs may provide low-cost medical care and testing services to members of the community, not just college students. However, one disadvantage to this type of center is that trainees with less experience will oversee a patient's care. Other resources available in some major cities are LGBTQ-focused medical centers. Overall, there will be more resources available to LGBTQ individuals in major metropolitan areas than in rural communities.

In some places, there are laws protecting transgender people from many forms of health-related discrimination. However, these laws and the protections they provide can vary widely from one jurisdiction to another. In the United States, there are states with legal protections for LGBTQ people that significantly exceed those offered by federal laws.

Health self-advocacy includes finding a doctor who understands your unique needs.

HEALTH SELF-ADVOCACY

Health self-advocacy is learning how to speak to your doctor about your needs, making your own health care decisions, and learning how to get information so you can make an informed decision about your health care.

Health self-advocacy includes finding a doctor who understands your unique needs and who will support your health care decisions. It also includes coming out to your doctor, so they can provide medical care that is personalized to your needs. For example, your doctor can refer you to specialists who are welcoming to LGBTQ people.

Health care is about treating the whole person. By being open with your doctor, they can provide you with the best-possible care, sensitive to current health trends affecting LGBTQ people. In some instances,

AIDS AND HIV IN MINORITY COMMUNITIES

Young, black, gay men are disproportionately affected by HIV/AIDS.

Sexually transmitted infections are a significant concern in certain LGBTQ groups. Gay men account for two-thirds of all people who are diagnosed with HIV each year, despite only making up an estimated 2 percent of U.S. population. Young, black, gay men are disproportionately affected, with the number of new HIV infections among this group rising 20 percent from 2008 to 2010. Research shows that the racial disparity in HIV incidence is due to lack of access to health care in non-white communities, not differences in sexual behavior. The few recent studies that look at HIV incidence in transgender populations reveal high HIV-infection rates. One systematic review estimated an HIV-infection rate of approximately 28 percent in transgender women in the United States.

LGBTQ people are afraid to come out to their medical provider. This fear can create stress, which in turn makes the need to divulge this information to their medical provider even more important. Taking the first step and coming out to your medical provider can require a leap of faith, but it is an essential stage in ensuring that LGBTQ people get the treatment they need to be healthy and happy as they live their authentic lives.

MENTAL HEALTH CONCERNS

Mental health is as an important of a component of healthy living as physical health. When someone has good mental health, they can function in society with minimal emotional and behavioral problems. A person with good mental health can think clearly, control their emotions, meet responsibilities and challenges, cope with daily life, and maintain healthy relationships with others.

While every person will experience emotional ups and downs because of life events they experience, most people function at a good level of mental health. There

There are cultural differences in how people handle stress.

Gay couples exploring HIV-prevention options to "Collect My Love" by The Knocks.

are cultural differences in how people handle stress. It is possible for people to have some areas of their life that are going well, and others that are falling apart. When it seems like more things are falling apart than going right, an individual may seek mental health treatment for a period of time.

LGBTQ people are three times more likely to experience major depression.

However, mental health conditions go beyond appropriate, everyday emotional reactions. They are medical conditions, just like heart disease or diabetes, and should be considered as such. Just like other diseases, mental health conditions can interfere with a person's daily life by changing how they think and feel. Because of this, it is essential that those who struggle with mental health conditions can receive the treatment they need. LGBTQ people deal with mental health concerns just like everyone else.

There are several mental health concerns that are more likely to occur in LGBTQ individuals due to the stigma and discrimination they experience. For example, LGBTQ people are three times more likely than the rest of the population to experience generalized anxiety disorder and major depression. In addition, the fear of coming out and being discriminated against for sexual orientation or gender identity can lead post-traumatic stress disorder, substance use disorder, and thoughts of suicide or self-harm. LGBTQ youth are also more likely to engage in unhealthy weight-control behaviors than their heterosexual peers.

LGBTQ people with mental illness must deal with the stigma of their sexual orientation or gender identity while also dealing with stigma of their mental health condition. This leads some people to hide their sexual orientation from their mental health care providers, because they fear being rejected or ridiculed, while it leads other people to hide their mental health condition from their LGBTQ friends for the same reasons.

The higher prevalence of mental health conditions in LGBTQ individuals is thought to come from the need to cope with **minority stress**. When an LGBTQ individual is also a member of another minority group, the likelihood that they will experience discrimination increases, as does the likelihood they will experience minority stress.

Learn more about Ali Forney's story.

HOMELESSNESS

LGBTQ people face unique challenges both in experiencing homelessness and when trying to avoid it. LGBTQ individuals who are homeless often have a hard time finding shelters that will accept them. They are also at a heightened risk of abuse, exploitation, and violence, compared to their heterosexual and cisgender counterparts.

Natalie became homeless at age 14 in a small town in Washington State. When her father left her family, her mother fell into a depression and started to use methamphetamine. According to Natalie, "[I]f she wasn't drunk or high, she was gone." Since Natalie had to care for her younger siblings when her mother was gone, she started missing school. Eventually, with no means to support her siblings and attend class at the same time, Natalie dropped out. As the stress of the situation continued to mount, she turned to using meth as a method of coping with the situation at home. This only made the conflict with her mother worse, and Natalie was kicked out of her mother's home.

Ali Forney

The Ali Forney Center serves the homeless LGBTQ youth living on the streets of New York City.

Ali Forney, at the age of 13, was a homeless gender-nonconforming youth who was forced to resort to sex work to survive. Despite his personal struggles, he educated anyone who would listen about HIV prevention and safe sex. Ali also pushed the NYPD to investigate a series of murders targeting members of the LGBTQ community. In December of 1997, his tragic murder on the streets of New York City called attention to the atrocious conditions for homeless LGBTQ youth. The Ali Forney Center was founded in 2002 to honor his memory. The Center is committed to making a difference in the lives of homeless LGBTQ youth living on the streets of New York City.

LGBTQ people face unique challenges both in experiencing homelessness and when trying to avoid it.

Natalie began to cycle between couch surfing and drug houses, exchanging sex with older men to have a place to sleep. By age 17, when addiction to meth had taken a strong hold, she found herself regularly returning to juvenile detention, where she was happy to have a safe place to sleep.

Adolescence is a period of many changes and an important period of development, and homeless youth such as Natalie are missing important opportunities for healthy teenage experiences and development. Because they do not have the necessary support to achieve a successful transition into adulthood, they are often prohibited from achieving their potential and making their special contributions to society.

The consequences of homelessness on LGBTQ youth can last a lifetime—it can have a negative impact on a person's mental and physical health. Youth who experience homelessness are at an increased risk for substance-abuse disorders, sexual abuse and exploitation, stigma, and discrimination. These youth also experience lower levels of educational

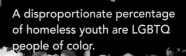

A disproportionate percentage of homeless youth are LGBTQ people of color.

♡ Please Help

Hey my name is Matt.
I'm 18 years old. I am
doing the best I can
with what I have.
Anything will help.
☮ THANK YOU ♡

attainment, which places them at a disadvantage in the job market. It is catastrophic to grow up without critical familial and social safety nets that teens rely on for educational attainment, economic stability, and life expectancy.

LGBTQ youth are at greater risk of becoming homeless due to family violence, rejection, and limited social support networks. One of the most commonly reported reasons that LGBTQ youth become homeless is being thrown out of the house by their parents after coming out. Research has found that 20 percent of young people leave their homes because their family disapproves of their sexual orientation or gender identity.

While a disproportionate percentage of homeless youth are LGBTQ people of color, many of the laws that have been put into place to serve the needs of the homeless fail to address their issues adequately. In addition to being homeless, LGBTQ youths who are also members of minority groups may find themselves losing the social support that had been provided by the larger community because of ejection from their households. Homeless youth live at the intersection of more than one marginalized identity, which may include their gender and identity expression, race, immigration status, ability, and more. The systems meant to help these youth often do not take their unique circumstances into account.

Homeless youth live at the intersection of more than one marginalized identity.

TEXT-DEPENDENT QUESTIONS

1. Why do some LGBTQ people not seek necessary medical care?

2. Why is homelessness a problem for LGBTQ youth?

3. What is health self-advocacy?

RESEARCH PROJECTS

1. Research local health insurance rules. Are there laws that prevent discrimination against LGBTQ people in your area?

2. Research a local organization that provides health care services to LGBTQ people. Was it difficult to locate? Do they charge for services?

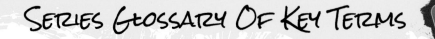

Agender (or neutrois, gender neutral, or genderless): Referring to someone who has little or no personal connection with gender.

Ally: Someone who supports equal civil rights, gender equality, and LGBTQ social movements; advocates on behalf of others; and challenges fear and discrimination in all its forms.

Asexual: An adjective used to describe people who do not experience sexual attraction. A person can also be aromantic, meaning they do not experience romantic attraction.

Asexual, or ace: Referring to someone who experiences little or no sexual attraction, or who experiences attraction but doesn't feel the need to act it out sexually. Many people who are asexual still identify with a specific sexual orientation.

Bigender: Referring to someone who identifies with both male and female genders, or even a third gender.

Binary: The belief that such things as gender identity have only two distinct, opposite, and disconnected forms. For example, the belief that only male and female genders exist. As a rejection of this belief, many people embrace a non-binary gender identity. (See **Gender nonconforming**.)

Biphobia: Fear of bisexuals, often based on stereotypes, including inaccurate associations with infidelity, promiscuity, and transmission of sexually transmitted infections.

Bisexual, or bi: Someone who is attracted to those of their same gender as well as to those of a different gender (for example, a woman who is attracted to both women and men). Some people use the word bisexual as an umbrella term to describe individuals that are attracted to more than one gender. In this way, the term is closely related to pansexual, or omnisexual, meaning someone who is attracted to people of any gender identity.

Butch, or masc: Someone whose gender expression is masculine. *Butch* is sometimes used as a derogatory term for lesbians, but it can also be claimed as an affirmative identity label.

Cisgender, or cis: A person whose gender identity matches the gender they were assigned at birth.

Coming out: The process through which a person accepts their sexual orientation and/or gender identity as part of their overall identity. For many, this involves sharing that identity with others, which makes it more of a lifetime process rather than just a one-time experience.

Cross-dresser: While anyone may wear clothes associated with a different sex, the term is typically used to refer to men who occasionally wear clothes, makeup, and accessories that are culturally associated with women. Those men typically identify as heterosexual. This activity is a form of gender expression and not done for entertainment purposes. Cross-dressers do not wish to permanently change their sex or live full-time as women.

Drag: The act of presenting as a different gender, usually for the purpose of entertainment (i.e., drag kings and queens). Many people who do drag do not wish to present as a different gender all of the time.

Gay: Someone who is attracted to those of their same gender. This is often used as an umbrella term but is used more specifically to describe men who are attracted to men.

Gender affirmation surgery: Medical procedures that some individuals elect to undergo to change their physical appearance to resemble more closely the way they view their gender identity.

Gender expression: The external manifestations of gender, expressed through such things as names, pronouns, clothing, haircuts, behavior, voice, and body characteristics.

Gender identity: One's internal, deeply held sense of gender. Some people identify completely with the gender they were assigned at birth (usually male or female), while others may identify with only a part of that gender or not at all. Some people identify with another gender entirely. Unlike gender expression, gender identity is not visible to others.

Gender nonconforming: Referring to someone whose gender identity and/or gender expression does not conform to the cultural or social expectations of gender, particularly in relation to male or female. This can be an umbrella term for many identities, including, but not limited to:

> **Genderfluid:** Someone whose gender identity and/or expression varies over time.

> **Genderqueer (or third gender):** Someone whose gender identity and/or expression falls between or outside of male and female.

Heterosexual: An adjective used to describe people whose enduring physical, romantic, and/ or emotional attraction is to people of the opposite sex. Also **straight**.

Homophobia: Fear of people who are attracted to the same sex. *Intolerance*, *bias*, or *prejudice* are usually more accurate descriptions of antipathy toward LGBTQ people.

Intergender: Referring to someone whose identity is between genders and/or a combination of gender identities and expressions.

Intersectionality: The idea that multiple identities intersect to create a whole that is different from its distinct parts. To understand someone, it is important to acknowledge that each of their identities is important and inextricably linked with all of the others. These can include identities related to gender, race, socioeconomic status, ethnicity, nationality, sexual orientation, religion, age, mental and/or physical ability, and more.

Intersex: Referring to someone who, due to a variety of factors, has reproductive or sexual anatomy that does not seem to fit the typical definitions for the female or male sex. Some people who are intersex may identify with the gender assigned to them at birth, while many others do not.

Lesbian: A woman who is attracted to other women. Some lesbians prefer to identify as gay women.

LGBTQ: Acronym for lesbian, gay, bisexual, transgender, and queer or questioning.

Non-binary and/or genderqueer: Terms used by some people who experience their gender identity and/or gender expression as falling outside the categories of man and woman. They may define their gender as falling somewhere in between man and woman, or they may define it as wholly different from these terms.

Out: Referring to a person who self-identifies as LGBTQ in their personal, public, and/or professional lives.

Pangender: Referring to a person whose identity comprises all or many gender identities and expressions.

Pride: The celebration of LGBTQ identities and the global LGBTQ community's resistance against discrimination and violence. Pride events are celebrated in many countries around the world, usually during the month of June to commemorate the Stonewall Riots that began in New York City in June 1969, a pivotal moment in the modern LGBTQ movement.

Queer: An adjective used by some people, particularly younger people, whose sexual orientation is not exclusively heterosexual (e.g., queer person, queer woman). Typically, for those who identify as queer, the terms *lesbian*, *gay*, and *bisexual* are perceived to be too limiting and/or fraught with cultural connotations that they feel don't apply to them. Some people may use *queer*, or more commonly *genderqueer*, to describe their gender identity and/or gender expression (see **non-binary** and/or **genderqueer**). Once considered a pejorative term, *queer* has been reclaimed by some LGBT people to describe themselves; however, it is not a universally accepted term, even within the LGBT community. When Q is seen at the end of LGBT, it may mean *queer* or *questioning*.

Questioning: A time in many people's lives when they question or experiment with their gender expression, gender identity, and/or sexual orientation. This experience is unique to everyone; for some, it can last a lifetime or be repeated many times over the course of a lifetime.

Sex: At birth, infants are commonly assigned a sex. This is usually based on the appearance of their external anatomy and is often confused with gender. However, a person's sex is actually a combination of bodily characteristics including chromosomes, hormones, internal and external reproductive organs, and secondary sex characteristics. As a result, there are many more sexes than just the binary male and female, just as there are many more genders than just male and female.

Sex reassignment surgery: See **Gender affirmation surgery**.

Sexual orientation: A person's enduring physical, romantic, and/or emotional attraction to another person. Gender identity and sexual orientation are not the same. Transgender people may be straight, lesbian, gay, bisexual, or queer. For example, a person who transitions from male to female and is attracted solely to men would typically identify as a straight woman.

Straight, or heterosexual: A word to describe women who are attracted to men and men who are attracted to women. This is not exclusive to those who are cisgender. For example, transgender men may identify as straight because they are attracted to women.

They/Them/Their: One of many sets of gender-neutral singular pronouns in English that can be used as an alternative to he/him/his or she/her/hers. Usage of this particular set is becoming increasingly prevalent, particularly within the LGBTQ community.

Transgender: An umbrella term for people whose gender identity and/or gender expression differs from what is typically associated with the sex they were assigned at birth. People under the transgender umbrella may describe themselves using one or more of a wide variety of terms— including transgender. A transgender identity is not dependent upon physical appearance or medical procedures.

Transgender man: People who were assigned female at birth but identify and live as a man may use this term to describe themselves. They may shorten it to *trans man*. Some may also use *FTM*, an abbreviation for *female-to-male*. Some may prefer to simply be called *men*, without any modifier. It is best to ask which term a person prefers.

Transgender woman: People who were assigned male at birth but identify and live as a woman may use this term to describe themselves. They may shorten it to *trans woman*. Some may also use *MTF*, an abbreviation for *male-to-female*. Some may prefer to simply be called *female*, without any modifier.

Transition: Altering one's birth sex is not a one-step procedure; it is a complex process that occurs over a long period of time. Transition can include some or all of the following personal, medical, and legal steps: telling one's family, friends, and co-workers; using a different name and new pronouns; dressing differently; changing one's name and/or sex on legal documents; hormone therapy; and possibly (though not always) one or more types of surgery. The exact steps involved in transition vary from person to person.

Transsexual: Someone who has undergone, or wishes to undergo, gender affirmation surgery. This is an older term that originated in the medical and psychological communities. Although many transgender people do not identify as transsexual, some still prefer the term.

Further Reading & Internet Resources

BOOKS

Crenshaw, Kimberlé. *On Intersectionality: Essential Writings.* The New Press, 2019.

A comprehensive and accessible introduction to the works of Kimberlé Crenshaw. This collection contains essays and articles that have defined intersectionality.

Mitchell, Saundra. *All Out: The No-Longer-Secret Stories of Queer Teens throughout the Ages.* Harlequin Teen, 2018.

Seventeen queer teens come together to create a collection of diverse historical fiction. From two girls falling in love while lamenting the death of Kurt Cobain, to a retelling of *Little Red Riding Hood* featuring a transgender soldier in war-torn 1870s Mexico, forbidden love in a Spanish convent, or an asexual girl finding out who she is while exploring the 1970s roller-disco scene, this book tells a wide range of stories from across cultures, time periods, and identities.

Vines, Matthew. *God and the Gay Christian: The Biblical Case in Support of Same-Sex Relationships.* Convergent Books, 2015.

As a faithful gay Christian, Matthew Vines explores what the Bible does and doesn't say about same-sex relationships.

WEB SITES

GLAAD. www.glaad.org
A national advocacy group dedicated to leading the conversation about equality for LGBTQ people. This organization works closely with the media to ensure that the public is provided powerful and true stories about the LGBTQ community in order to advocate for equality.

GLSEN. www.glsen.org
A small, dedicated group of teachers founded the group in 1990 to improve an education system that frequently overlooks LGBTQ students who are bullied or discriminated against, or fall through the cracks. Today, it is the leading national organization for ensuring safe and affirming schools for LGBTQ students. The organization conducts extensive and original research, authors developmentally appropriate resources, works with policy makers to ensure inclusive school policies, and empowers students to affect change in their own communities.

GSA Network. www.gsanetwork.org
GSA clubs (originally called "Gay–Straight Alliance clubs" when they were established in the 1980s) are student-run organizations in both high schools and middle schools that provide support and activism activities to LGBTQ youth. The overarching goal of GSA clubs is to empower students to support each other and talk about issues related to sexual identity and gender identity and expression.

Human Rights Campaign. www.hrc.org
HRC is the largest organization advocating for the civil rights of lesbian, gay, bisexual, and transgender Americans, with more than 3 million members and supporters nationwide. The organization also educates the public on LGBTQ issues and offers a number of research publications outlining equality indexes on areas such as health care, employers, and states.

It Gets Better Project. www.itgetsbetter.org
The nonprofit It Gets Better Project, founded in 2010, exists to uplift, empower, and connect LGBTQ youth around the globe. The Project includes more than 50,000 video messages from people of all sexual orientations and gender identities, including many celebrities, reassuring young people who face bullying and harassment that life does indeed get better.

Index

AUTHORS' BIOGRAPHIES

Rebecca Kaplan (a disabled bisexual woman) and Avery Kaplan (a transgender woman) are a queer couple living in Orange County, California. Rebecca has a Master of Science degree in criminology and criminal justice from San Diego State University, and both women earned a Juris Doctor degree from Chapman University's Dale E. Fowler School of Law.

CREDITS

COVER

(clockwise from top left) iStock/SoumenNath; iStock/Rawpixel; iStock/Rawpixel; iStock/Rawpixel

INTERIOR